# Vegan Start
# Passover Cookbook

by

## Rena Reich

# CONTENT

Hello there. This is the second edition of the Vegan Passover Cookbook. I had such a wonderful response to the first edition that I thought I would update and add to it. I hope you enjoy using it as much as I enjoyed writing it.

I have been a vegan now for over 6 years. As the years go by, it becomes easier and easier to maintain a vegan lifestyle. Especially living in Israel. When I started being vegan there was practically no place to eat out unless you wanted to eat a green salad. Wow has that changed. Now, practically every chain restaurant has real vegan options, and they are all marked on the menu.

Besides eating out, more and more vegan foods are being produced and imported than ever before. (The one thing that I still miss is hot dogs. I make my own, but there is nothing like the convenience of just pulling hot dogs out of the fridge.)

That being said, Passover can still be difficult. That's OK. I'm here to help.

I like to cook. More than I like to cook, I like to eat food that tastes good. One thing that is very important to me is that I have good food for my family to eat, especially during the holiday. No one goes hungry in my house. Follow these recipes and no one will go hungry in your house either.

# SHOPPING LIST

These are things that I buy before Passover starts. Don't worry about buying too much, these are things you can use all year long.

### Basics:

- Wine
- Matzo
- Matzo Meal
- Matzo Cake Meal
- Potato Starch
- Canola Oil
- Olive Oil
- Coconut Oil
- Margarine
- Vegetable Oil Spray
- Red Wine Vinegar
- Vinegar
- Baking Soda
- Baking Powder
- Apple Sauce
- Salt
- Kosher Salt
- Sugar
- Brown Sugar
- Coconut Flakes
- Chocolate Chips
- Cocoa Powder
- Silan (Date Honey)
- Maple Syrup
- Agave Syrup
- Vanilla
- Raspberry Preserves
- Tomato Paste

### Fruits and Veggies:

- Potatoes
- Sweet Potatoes
- Onions
- Garlic
- Carrots
- Celery
- Zucchini
- Beets
- Mushrooms (all kinds)
- Pepper
- Tomatoes
- Cucumbers
- Lettuce
- Spinach
- Parsley
- Apples
- Pears
- Bananas
- Lemons
- Dried Cranberries
- Dates
- Whatever I can find that is in season and looks good.

### Nuts:

- Almonds
- Walnuts
- Macadamia Nuts
- Pecans

### Spices:

- Paprika (make sure that it is not made with oil that contains kitniyot)
- Hot Paprika
- Thyme
- Cinnamon
- Nutmeg
- Ginger
- Salt
- Pepper

# SEDER

Our Seder is pretty normal. We go through the Haggadah, we take turns reading and we sing all the songs. The only things that are a bit different are some of the things we use on our Seder plate.

**Maror:** Bitter herbs. We use romaine lettuce, but you can use horseradish. It is meant to symbolize the bitterness that we endured when we were slaves in Egypt.

**Charoset:** Nut and fruit paste. This symbolizes the bricks and mortar that we were forced to use when we were slaves. It reminds us of the hard labor.

**Chazeret:** More bitter herbs. We use romaine lettuce here too. It's used to make the sandwich for the Korech part of the Seder.

**Karpas:** Dipping vegetable. We use parsley or celery for this. You are supposed to dip it in salt water. This represents the tears that we cried when we were slaves.

**Zeroah:** Shank bone. This is where it starts getting a bit tricky to be vegan. We use roasted beets. There is actually a source for using beets: Pesachim 114b. It's supposed to symbolize the Paschal Lamb that was sacrificed before we left Egypt.

**Beitzah:** Roasted boiled egg. We usually just leave it out. It is supposed to symbolize the sacrifices that we offered during the second temple. It's also a circle, which symbolizes life. I've asked around what other people do for this. Some people use an avocado pit. Others use a white eggplant. The most inventive one that I've heard to date is using a plastic egg. I actually really like that one. We may be doing it this year – if I can find a plastic egg.

The thing to remember about the Seder plate is that it is there to represent things to us. The beitzah and the zeroah don't even get eaten. These are traditional things that we use, but what's important is what they represent to us.

Vegan Start

# OUR SEDER MEAL

Every year I look for new and interesting things to make for Passover, but the main Seder meal stays more or less the same.

- Mock Chopped Liver
- Vegetable Soup with Matzo Balls
- Mushroom Steaks
- Potato Kugel
- Tzimmes
- Spinach Salad
- Chocolate Torte

I try to keep Seder night pretty simple. After eating all that Matzo, it's practically a sin to eat this much. Somehow we do it.

# SAUCES AND SPREADS

Before we get into the real food, let's start with sauces and spreads. These are things that I make at the beginning, before the holiday starts and we have throughout the week.

I put my charoset recipe here too. We eat it on Seder night and we keep on enjoying it throughout the week. I hope you enjoy it too.

# CHAROSET

 5 minutes

## Ingredients:

- **walnuts - 1 cup**
- **dates - 8, pitted**
- **apple - 1 peeled**
- **cinnamon - 1 teaspoon**
- **sweet red wine - 1/2 cup**

## Instructions:

1. **Peel and core apple**
2. **Place all the ingredients  a blender**
3. **Blend**

Charoset represents the mortar that held together the brick the Jewish people used to create great cities for Pharaoh and the Egyptians. When my mother makes charoset, it always comes out chunky style. I prefer creamy. I think the symbolism works better that way.

We make charoset for Seder night, but we like to eat it after the Seder as well. It's a really sweet, yummy paste. It's more like a dessert than a sandwich filler. The amount that you need for Seder is really minimal. That means that there is a decent amount left over for lunch the next day. Yum!

The charoset that I grew up with didn't have dates. The dates don't only add to the sweetness, they also make the charoset more mortar like.

# ALMOND MILK

 5 minutes

## Ingredients:

- raw almonds - 1 cup
- dates - 3
- water - 2 cups
- vanilla - 1/2 teaspoon

## Instructions:

*If you are using blanched almonds:*
1. Soak almonds overnight

*If you use unblanched almonds:*
2. Soak almonds in hot water for 2 hours
3. Skin will be loose - remove from almonds.If they don't come off easily, soak a bit more.

*For everyone:*
4. Put ingredients in a blender and blend well
5. Pour through cheese cloth

*After the almond milk is made, take the leftover almonds and dry them out in the oven on low heat until they are completely dried out. Store in the freezer until you are ready to use it.*

One of the things that I love about making almond milk is that you don't just get milk. You get finely grated almonds that you can use in a ton of different things. After I dry out the leftover almonds, I can grind them again. That makes it fine enough to use as a flour, or I can just use them as is.

You can use regular raw almonds or blanched. It's not a huge deal to use regular, but it does take time to remove the skins.

I'll make almond milk a few times the week of Passover. I use it in a ton of recipes.

# MAYONNAISE

 **5 minutes**

## Ingredients:

- **almond milk - 1/2 cup**
- **olive oil - 1/4 cup**
- **ripe avocado - 3 tablespoons**
- **lemon juice - 1/2 teaspoon**
- **salt - 1/4 teaspoon**

## Instructions:

1. **Blend all the ingredients together**
2. **Refrigerate to thicken**

I like mayonnaise. I know it's not the healthiest thing in the world, which is why it tastes so good. It makes such a difference in a lot of salads. It's true that you can use olive oil in salads like potato salad, but they're just so much better with mayo! I have been making vegan mayonnaise for a long time. During the year I use soy milk which makes a very nice thick mayonnaise. Almond milk doesn't work the same. The taste may be the same with almond milk, but it comes out too runny. I've modified my original recipe to make it thicker.

# ALMOND BUTTER

 **5 minutes**

## Ingredients:

- almonds - 2 cups
- oil - 2 tablespoons
- salt - 1/2 teaspoon
- date honey - 1 tablespoon

## Instructions:

1. Place almonds and oil in a blender and blend until creamy
2. Add salt and date honey and process until combined
3. Done

I love peanut butter. It's one of those foods that I miss when Pesach comes around. A couple of years ago I saw almond butter, Kosher for Passover, being sold in the store. I tried it, but it was so greasy and laden with sugar that it was inedible. So I decided to make my own. It's so easy to make, I won't be spending another Passover without it.

Almond butter is great on apples. It's also great as a Pesach substitute for peanut butter. It works very well with jelly on matzo.

# PESTO

 **5 minutes**

**Ingredients:**

- **fresh basil - 1 package**
- **garlic - 2 cloves**
- **olive oil - 1/4 cup**
- **salt - 1/2 teaspoon**

**Instructions:**

1. **Wash and dry basil**
2. **Place all ingredients in a blender**
3. **Process until smooth**

This is another great spread that is crazy easy to make. For Passover, I use walnuts. During the year, I use pine nuts. There is not much of a difference in taste, but I think that the pine nuts make it a bit creamier.

If you want to use it on pasta, add a bit of olive oil to thin it down.

# MATBUCHA

 **50 minutes**      **10 minutes**

## Ingredients:

- **bell peppers - 3, multiple colors**
- **tomatoes - 3 large**
- **garlic - 2 cloves**
- **onion - 1 large, chopped**
- **salt - 1/2 teaspoon**
- **paprika - 1 teaspoon**
- **olive oil - 2 tablespoons**

## Instructions:

1. **Roast the peppers in the oven or on the fire, turning as necessary, until they are black on all sides**
2. **Place in a paper bag and let cool**
3. **Boil tomatoes in their skins until they float**
4. **Remove skins from peppers and tomatoes**
5. **Heat oil and add onions and garlic until translucent**
6. **Chop peppers and add to onions and garlic**
7. **Add tomatoes and mash with a fork**
8. **Add salt and paprika and simmer for 10 minutes**
9. **Serve warm or cold**

Matbucha is easy enough to get year round in the supermarket. For Pesach, it's really hard to find one that doesn't have kitniyot, so I make it myself.

Although it's a bit of work, it really is fun to do. There really is no comparison between the stuff that you get in the store and the stuff you make yourself. I like to put the peppers directly on the fire and watch them turn black. You can roast them in the oven too, but it has a better flavor when you do it on the range.

This is a no-alarm recipe for matbucha. Feel free to add spicy peppers or chili powder if you want to give it more kick.

# BABA GHANOUSH

 5 minutes    40 minutes

## Ingredients:

- eggplant - 1 large
- vegan mayonnaise - 1/4 cup
- garlic - 2 cloves, chopped finely
- salt - 1/2 teaspoon

## Instructions:

1. Prick eggplant with a knife and roast it in the oven, turning it so that it is blackened on all sides
2. Let cool
3. Cut in half and scrape out the insides of the eggplant
4. Drain excess liquid
5. Add the rest of the ingredients and mix thoroughly
6. Serve chilled

This is also known as eggplant salad. I've eaten eggplant salad for years. Once when I was at my cousins in Huntington they served baba ghanoush. I had no idea what it was until I tasted it. With the fancy name, it still tasted great.

I like making it with mayonnaise that I make myself, but you can make it with tahini (during the year – it's kitniyot on Pesach) if you like that better. It's a stronger flavor and not quite as creamy.

After you roast the eggplant, it is really easy to scrape out the insides with a fork. The eggplant gives off a lot of water. Make sure to drain it well so that your baba ghanoush isn't runny.

# ALMOND CRACKERS

 15 minutes        🕐 20 minutes

## Ingredients:

- almond pulp - 2 3/4 cups
- matzo meal - 1/2 cup, finely ground
- salt - 2 teaspoons
- olive oil - 4 tablespoons
- water - 3/4 cup
- rosemary - 1 tablespoon, ground

## Instructions:

1. Heat oven to 450 degrees
2. Mix dry ingredients
3. Add oil and water and mix into a dough
4. Roll so that it is about 1/8th inch thick
5. Brush with water and sprinkle with rosemary
6. Slice into cracker size pieces and place on a lined baking sheet
7. Prick with a fork and bake for 15-20 minutes
8. Cool and store in a dry container

You can blame this recipe on raw cookbooks. While looking through them, I got inspired to make almond crackers. Their recipes use flaxseeds and a dehydrator. I don't use either on Pesach. When I roll these out, I put them between 2 baking sheets. If you don't have a rolling pin for Pesach, feel free to mush them down with the heel of your palm.

Use the almond pulp left over from making almond milk. If you don't have any, feel free to use real almonds. Grind almonds into a fine powder with your blender.

# ROASTED GARLIC SPREAD

 5 minutes      1 hour

## Ingredients:

- garlic - 1 head
- olive oil - 2 tablespoons
- Kosher salt - ½ teaspoon

## Instructions:

1. Heat oven to 400 degrees
2. Cut the top off of the head of garlic
3. Place on cookie sheet
4. Drench with olive oil
5. Sprinkle with salt
6. Roast for 30-35 minutes, until cloves are soft
7. When cool, peel garlic
8. Blend until smooth

I made Aliya (moved to Israel) when I was 20. I didn't have a lot of family in the country when I moved here, but the ones that I did have were amazingly warm and helped me out in every way that they could.

Before I figured out what I was going to do with my life, I lived at Avrum and Rivka's house. I spent many wonderful Shabbats with them even after I finally figured it out. Naturally I went to them for Passover when it rolled around. Rivka's father (z"l) didn't like to use butter or jam on his matzo. Instead he would take cloves of garlic and just rub them on his matzo and eat it. I tried it myself a few times. It was a bit sharp for me, but it tasted really good.

Reminiscing a bit, I decided to try roasting the garlic and making a spread of it. I've kept it very simple. It really doesn't need anything else.

# PASSOVER BISCUITS

 10 minutes    50 minutes

## Ingredients:

- matzo cake meal - 2 1/2 cups
- baking powder - 2 tablespoons
- salt - 1 teaspoon
- water - 1 cup
- oil - 1/4 cup

## Instructions:

1. Heat oven to 300 degrees
2. Mix the dry ingredients together
3. Add the wet ingredients and mix well the consistency should be like play dough
4. Separate the dough into 6 and roll into balls
5. Score the tops of the rolls with a knife
6. Bake 50 minutes

It may be politically incorrect to say this, but sometimes I get sick of eating matzo all the time. Instead of complaining about matzo (OK, in addition to complaining about matzo), I came up with an alternative.

They're great for breakfast, or as a snack. I like them with pesto. My husband prefers them with jam or margarine.

# FARMER'S CHEESE

 **120 minutes**      **20 minutes**

## Ingredients:

- almond milk - 1 3/4 cups (1 recipe)
- vinegar - 3 teaspoons

## Instructions:

1. Bring milk to boil
2. Lower heat and slowly add vinegar
3. Let cook down for 10 minutes, stirring occasionally
4. Strain through a cheese cloth for a couple of hours

As a special treat, I like to make blintzes for Passover. I make crepes and fill them with a mixture of farmer's cheese, raisins, vanilla and sugar. It really takes me back to my Savta Sadie cooking in the kitchen. She was a real Balabusta (Yiddish for homemaker, but it means so much more). I may never reach her level of Balabustahood, but I'd like to think that I make her proud by making my family blintzes. And it all starts with the farmer's cheese.

# BREAKFAST

Why should this holiday be different than any other holiday? I am always looking for a reason to make pancakes. Having everyone home is the perfect reason. Pancakes and matzo brei are breakfast staples in our house for Passover.

# MATZO MEAL PANCAKES

 5 minutes         30 minutes

## Ingredients:

- matzo meal - 1 1/2 cups
- sugar - 1/4 cup
- baking powder - 4 teaspoons
- water - 3 cups
- oil - 1/2 cup
- apple sauce - 1/2 cup
- cinnamon - 1 teaspoon

## Instructions:

1. Mix all ingredients together
2. Lightly oil frying pan
3. Pour heaping tablespoons of batter on hot frying pan and flatten out batter
4. Let cook for 2 minutes, until pancakes brown
5. Carefully flip and let cook on second side another 2 minutes
6. Serve warm with maple syrup

I make pancakes a lot during the year. It just seems wrong not to make them on Passover as well. These pancakes are not the light and fluffy ones that we have during the rest of the year. Why aren't they? So the children should ask? Not really. Matzo meal is much heavier than regular flour. No matter - they still taste great with a bit of maple syrup.

This batter is very thick. After you spoon it out, make sure to flatten it out so that it will cook through. You can wet a spoon if you find it's too sticky to flatten out any other way.

# MATZO BREI

 15 minutes     20 minutes

## Ingredients:

- matzo - 10 pieces
- water - for soaking
- potato starch - 3 heaping tablespoons
- salt - 1 teaspoon
- oil - for frying

## Instructions

1. Break matzo into small pieces
2. Cover with water and wait 5 minutes
3. Drain excess water
4. Add potato starch and salt, and mix well
5. Heat oil in a frying pan
6. Add some of mixture to frying pan so that it's about an inch think (it needs to be cooked in batches)
7. Wait about a minute, until it starts to brown, and flip with a spatula
8. Cook on the second side another minute
9. Serve

In my family, it isn't Pesach without Matzo Brei. This is something that has been made for generations in my family. As a kid, we would wake up the first day of Pesach and steaming hot Matzo Brei would be waiting for us. We always put sugar and cinnamon on ours. It wasn't until years later that I found out that people use pepper and salt. That just seemed so strange to me. I guess its different strokes for different folks.

The Matzo Brei that my mother and grandmother made was full of eggs. What keeps this Matzo Brei together is potato starch and patience. You need to let it cook on each side for a minute before you flip it over.

# CREPES

 10 minutes     20 minutes

## Ingredients:

- matzo cake meal - 1 cup
- potato starch - 1/2 cup
- baking powder - 1 teaspoon
- salt - 1/2 teaspoon
- almond milk - 2 1/2 cups
- oil - 1 cup

## Instructions:

1. Mix dry ingredients together
2. Add wet ingredients and mix well, removing all lumps
3. Let batter sit for 5 minutes
4. Heat crepe pan on medium heat
5. Spoon 1/2 cup mixture on crepe pan and rotate the pan to spread evenly
6. Fry on one side, lifting corners of crepe so that it doesn't stick
7. When crepe looks dry, flip in pan and let cook about 1/2 a minute longer
8. Flip onto plate and repeat the process until batter is done

I have been trying to get this recipe right for years. My Savta Sadie z"l was the best crepe maker in the world. When we spent Passover together, she would be like a machine and flip these babies out one after the other, with great precision. All her crepes came out perfectly.

Making a vegan version was very difficult. You use too much matzo cake meal and they come out too thick. You use too much potato starch and they come out too sticky. You need to add enough oil or they stick to the pan. You need to be a little patient or they come out too thin (before the matzo meal has time to set properly).

These are plain crepes. You can fill them with fruit or almond farmers cheese and raisins with a bit of vanilla and sugar or fried onions and mashed potatoes (if you want to go savory). You can also just sprinkle some cinnamon and sugar on them and eat them as they are the way my Savta used to serve them. The choices are endless.

# SOUPS

We are a family that is heavy on soups. Besides the two that I make every Shabbat, we often have soup during the week. Passover is no different.

You can get soup almonds that are Kosher for Passover and are not made with eggs. (I'm not sure that I want to know what they are made of.) We usually just break matzo into our soup and have a good time with it.

# VEGETABLE SOUP

 20 minutes    🕐 2 hours

## Ingredients:

- olive oil - 2 tablespoons
- onion - 1 large, chopped
- garlic - 2 cloves, chopped
- mushrooms - 4 large, chopped
- carrots - 2, chopped
- celery - 2 stalks, chopped
- zucchini - 2, chopped
- sweet potato - 1 large, chopped
- parve chicken soup bouillon - 3 tablespoons
- water - 10 cups

## Instructions:

1. In a large soup pot, heat oil
2. Add onion, garlic, mushrooms, carrots and celery and cook until onions are translucent
3. Add zucchini and sweet potatoes and cook another 5 minutes
4. Add the rest of the ingredients and bring to boil
5. Lower flame and let cook for about an hour
6. Serve hot

This is a soup that I make on a regular basis. If you know how to use a potato peeler, then this soup is easy to make. I make my matzo balls right in the soup. If you leave a couple of matzo balls in, they will disintegrate in the soup and make it thicker. Sometimes I do it on purpose and sometimes by accident. Either way, it comes out good.

This is Jewish soul food.

# MATZO BALLS

 **60 minutes**        **30 minutes**

## Ingredients:

- **matzo meal - 1 cup**
- **potato starch - 3 tablespoons**
- **oil - 1/4 cup**
- **water - 1 cup**
- **baking soda - 1/2 teaspoon**
- **salt - 1/4 teaspoon**
- **garlic - 1/4 teaspoon**

## Instructions:

1. **Mix all ingredients together**
2. **Refrigerate for 1/2 hour**
3. **Roll into balls and place in boiling soup**
4. **Simmer in soup until they grow (about 20 minutes)**
5. **Take out of soup with a slotted spoon and let harden for 30 minutes to 1 hour**
6. **Put the balls back in the soup about 1/2 hour before it's ready to be served to heat up**
7. **Serve**

I think that matzo ball soup has to be one of the most traditional foods around. I couldn't imagine a Passover Seder without them. That's why I went on a mission to figure out how to make them egg-free. These babies are also kitniyot-free (no legumes). I started trying to figure out what I could use to fluff matzo balls up and keep them together. Eggs are a very important part of the original recipe. By adding baking soda and potato starch I was able to come pretty close to the original. They are more delicate, but they taste the same.

If you don't take the balls out of the soup, they will fall apart. Taking them out gives them a chance to get firm. Once they have firmed up, you can put them back in the soup without any fears.

I actually figured out the part about taking them out to let them harden by accident. In one of my attempts, I decided to get rid of a batch because they were falling apart. They tasted good, so I just put them on the side to try to figure out what to do with them. When I had a chance to get back to them, they were the perfect consistency. I love a story with a happy ending.

While testing out this recipe, on one of the rounds I used olive oil. I personally feel that olive oil has too strong a flavor. I use canola oil, but any light oil should do.

# ORANGE (PUMPKIN) SOUP

 25 minutes      2 hours

## Ingredients:

- olive oil - 2 tablespoons
- green onions - 1 large, chopped
- carrots - 2 large, chopped
- celery stalk - 2 large, chopped
- zucchini - 2 large, chopped
- sweet potatoes - 1 large (about 2 cups) chopped
- pumpkin - 4 cups, chopped
- parve chicken soup bouillon - 3 tablespoons
- water - to almost cover

## Instructions:

1. Heat oil
2. Add vegetable, one at a time until all are cooked
3. Add water to almost cover
4. Add bouillon and boil until vegetables are soft
5. Let cool and process with hand blender
6. Reheat and serve warm

This soup is called orange soup, but it has no oranges in it. The first time that I was offered this soup I didn't know what to expect. It's called orange because of the color, which it gets from the orange vegetables in it. It works a lot better in Hebrew than in English. Katom is the color orange and Tapuz is the fruit. I hope that you enjoy this Marak Katom!

I chop all the vegetables while I make this soup.

I start with the onions and let them cook while I peel and chop the carrots. By the time I get to the pumpkin, all the other vegetables are nicely cooked and it takes only a couple of minutes to finish it up. The vegetables let off liquid, so you shouldn't need to add more oil.

My hand blender is my favorite kitchen appliance. I love using it for all kinds of soups. It makes them come out nice and creamy.

# BORSCHT

 20 minutes       2 hours

**Ingredients:**

- oil - 2 tablespoons
- onion - 1 large
- garlic - 2 cloves, chopped
- carrots - 2, chopped into cubes
- beets - 3, chopped into cubes
- parve chicken soup bouillon - 2 tablespoon
- water - 5 cups

**Instructions:**

1. Heat up oil
2. Add onions, garlic and carrots and cook on a medium heat until onions are translucent
3. Add beets and cook a bit more
4. Add water and bouillon and cook until beets are soft
5. Serve warm

I used to hate beets growing up. I'm not sure why. Perhaps it was that I associated beets as old people's food. My kids love beets and they're not old, so I guess I was wrong all those years... My mom would always try to get me to try them, but I was really stubborn about them.

I use fresh beets. It can get a bit messy. I sometimes wear plastic gloves so that the red beet juice doesn't stain my hands while I'm peeling and chopping the veggies.

This is a very simple recipe that is fast and easy to make. When the soup is done, you can't tell the carrots from the beets, but believe me, they are still there.

# POTATO LEEK SOUP

 20 minutes  2 hours

## Ingredients:

- olive oil - 4 tablespoons
- leeks - 3 large, chopped
- potatoes - 6 large, chopped
- parve chicken soup bouillon - 3 tablespoons
- water - 10 cups

## Instructions:

1. Heat oil
2. Add leeks and cook until translucent
3. Add potatoes and cook for a couple of more minutes, stirring often
4. Add the rest of the ingredients and bring to a boil
5. Lower flame and cook until potatoes are soft
6. Remove from flame and process roughly with a hand blender
7. Serve warm

Soups are one of those great foods that fill you up, keep you warm, and are easy to make. Especially this nice thick soup. I like to make this during the week of Chol Hamoed Pesach.

Having a hand blender is crucial to my happiness on Pesach. I like to blend this soup halfway so that it's a bit chunky. If you don't have a hand blender, try a potato masher, or putting half of the soup in a regular food processor. Those work too, but aren't quite as easy.

Classic potato leek soup uses butter for frying the leeks. Frying the leeks in olive oil gives a lovely, rich flavor. I actually like it better.

# CREAM OF MUSHROOM SOUP

 **15 minutes**    **2 hours**

## Ingredients:

- olive oil - 2 tablespoons
- onion - 1 large, chopped
- mushrooms - 1 1/2 cartons, chopped
- garlic - 2 cloves, chopped
- potato starch - 3 tablespoons
- parve chicken soup bouillon - 2 tablespoons
- almond milk - 2 cups
- water - 2 cups
- salt - to taste

## Instructions:

1. Heat oil in the bottom of a soup pot
2. Add onions, mushrooms and garlic, and cook on a medium heat, until mushrooms are translucent
3. Add potato starch and mix to create a paste
4. Slowly add the liquid to break up the potato starch mixture
5. Add the rest of the ingredients and bring to a boil
6. Lower heat and cook 20 minutes longer
7. Serve warm

Mushrooms have to be my favorite food ever. I don't really know how they come into being, but I'm so glad that they are here.

Cream of mushroom soup was always something that we bought. I never thought of making it myself until recently. The idea of cooking with milk is not something that I was brought up on. Besides that, the Israeli soy milk is a bit too sweet to use and is not really the best thing for cooking. I like to use almond milk that I make myself for this recipe. It gives the smoothness without the sweetness.

All types of mushrooms work for this soup. I use the regular, button mushrooms. If you want a stronger mushroom flavor, try shitake.

# SIDES AND SALADS

This is the vegan food that most people understand. Everyone expects us to just eat veggies all week. I go a bit further with it. I make kugels that are completely egg-free. They are just as good as their egg-laden brothers. You will be fooled.

# ROASTED BEETS

 **20 minutes**     **60 minutes**

## Ingredients:

- **Beets**

## Instructions:

1. **Heat oven to 400 degrees**
2. **Cut off green tops and the pointy bottom of the beet**
3. **Wash thoroughly**
4. **Prick beets with a fork**
5. **Wrap in tinfoil**
6. **Bake for 45 - 60 minutes, until you can pierce it easily with a fork**
7. **Let beets cool a bit**
8. **Hold beets in paper towel and rub away the skin (if it doesn't peel away easily, the beets need to be cooked longer)**
9. **Slice and use**

When I was a kid I hated beets. My mother would try to get me to eat them, but I would hold my nose up and walk away. I think the real turnoffs were their texture and how they stained everything.

As a grownup, I love beets. I make salads and soups with them all the time. I don't even need to do that much to them. I just roast them and sprinkle a bit of salt, and then I have a nice snack. Instead of the shank bone for our Seder Plate, we use roasted beets. We aren't the only ones that do it either. There is a source in the Talmud for using beets. Just look up Pesachim, 114b. When peeling the beets, I wear disposable rubber gloves so I don't stain my hands. It's no fun going to seder looking red handed.

# KISHKE

 **15 minutes**

## Ingredients:

- **onion - 1 large, grated**
- **carrots - 2, grated**
- **celery stalk - 1 stalk, grated**
- **oil - 3/4 cup**
- **salt - 2 teaspoons**
- **paprika - 1 teaspoon**
- **matzo meal - 1 1/2 cups**

## Instructions:

1. **In a food processor, shred onion, carrots and celery.**
2. **In a bowl, add processed vegetables and the rest of the ingredients.**
3. **Wrap in tin foil.**
4. **Add to cholent or bake in the oven at 350 degrees for 40 minutes**

I think that I should write a whole book just on Jewish soul food. When talking about comfort foods, there is nothing more comforting than waking up on Shabbat morning to the aroma of cholent with mock kishke cooking inside. The smell wafts through the house. It really brings back some wonderful childhood memories.

What is kishke? I'm not sure that anyone really wants to know. It's some sort of dough mixture stuffed into cow intestines. After that description, I'm sure that you're thinking "yum." Well it's really a lot better than it sounds. The mock version uses tin foil instead of the intestines to hold the mixture together. So you get all the taste with none of the intestines. I promise you that no animals were hurt in the production of my kishke.

You can cook it in the oven, but I really like to put it in cholent. It comes out so moist and flavorful. The kids totally devour it. It may sound weird, but it's really worth giving it a try.

# MOCK CHOPPED LIVER

 20 minutes

### Ingredients:

- mushrooms - 2 cups
- onions - 2 large, chopped
- oil - for frying
- walnuts - 1 cup
- salt - to taste
- pepper - to taste

### Instructions:

1. Heat about 2 tablespoons of oil in fry pan
2. Add onions and mushrooms and cook on a medium heat until caramelized. Add oil as needed
3. Put walnuts in a food processor and process
4. Add caramelized onions and mushrooms and process until smooth
5. Mix in salt and pepper to taste
6. Eat

I was so happy when I found this recipe. I've made other mock chop livers before – with peas or string beans, but those all had hard boiled eggs in them. No good for me.

This is one of my favorite recipes. You can serve it warm or cold.

# CAULIFLOWER POPPERS

 10 minutes    30 minutes

## Ingredients:

- cauliflower - 1 large head (frozen can also be used)
- garlic powder - 1 tablespoon
- chili powder - 1 teaspoon
- paprika - 1 1/2 teaspoon
- salt - 1/2 teaspoon
- vegetable oil spray

## Instructions:

- Cut up cauliflower into bite-size pieces and place in large Ziploc bag
- Sprinkle in all of the spices and shake until the cauliflower is evenly coated
- Spray a baking sheet with vegetable spray and place the cauliflower on it
- Bake at 400 degrees for about a 1/2 hour, or until cauliflower is cooked through
- Serve warm

All veggies are Kosher for Passover, and with the exception of beans and corn, most aren't kitniyot, so I can serve them to anyone that walks into my house.

I've been making cauliflower poppers for years. What I really love about them is how simple they are. I also love that the kids can't stop eating them. It's really nice to be able to make something with such a wide appeal. I'll make a batch and by the time dinner comes around, there are practically none left because they've all been noshed away. So if you're going to make them, you might as well make a double batch.

I really don't think that you can get much easier than this recipe. The hardest thing is cutting up the cauliflower, and although I've often told my husband that I'd like a sous chef for my birthday (I find constant cutting a drag and time consuming), this is really not that bad.

I like to use fresh cauliflower, but in a pinch, frozen works well too. You just need to cook it a bit longer so that it's not soggy. It used to be impossible to get fresh cauliflower here, but now we get it all the time.

Another really nice thing about this recipe is that it's practically fat-free and has practically no calories. Since Passover is all about freedom, this really fits the bill. I really love recipes like this one because it makes my vegan Passover a whole lot less scary. Isn't that what freedom is all about?

# CARROT KUGEL

 15 minutes       60 minutes

**Ingredients:**

- **carrots - 3 cups, grated**
- **apple sauce - 1 cup**
- **date honey - 1/2 cup**
- **oil - 1/2 cup**
- **matzo meal - 1 1/2 cups, finely ground**
- **baking powder - 1 tablespoon**
- **cinnamon - 1 teaspoon**

**Instructions:**

1. **Mix all the ingredients together**
2. **Oil a baking pan**
3. **Pour into the baking pan**
4. **Bake at 350 degrees for 50-60 minutes**

When I was working more than full time outside of the house, we used to buy Passover food. The kids were little and life was a lot more hectic and traveling every day zapped all my energy. I don't remember the name of the place that we used, but I do remember having amazing carrot kugel.

I'm sure that their kugel was laden with eggs. I've tried to replicate the flavor here.

Depending on the size of your carrots, 5 or 6 carrots peeled and grated should do the trick. Feel free to add some raisins if you like them.

# POTATO KUGEL

 15 minutes      60 minutes

## Ingredients:

- potatoes - 5 large
- onion - 1 large
- oil - 1/2 cup
- potato starch - 1/4 cup
- matzo meal - 1/4 cup
- salt - 1 1/2 teaspoons
- pepper - pinch

## Instructions:

1. Peel potatoes
2. Grate potatoes and onion
3. Add the rest of the ingredients and mix well
4. Pour into baking pan and bake at 350 degrees for an hour
5. Serve warm

Practically every Shabbat mevarchim (the Shabbat that is before a new Jewish month begins) my friend organizes a Kiddush. He always makes potato kugel. He's not vegan, but for me, he makes it vegan. When I asked him for his recipe, he could tell me what was in it, but not the amounts of anything. He just does it by feel.

I've played around with the recipe and I've come up with my own amounts. I'm pleased with it. The beauty of this recipe is that it is naturally Kosher for Passover. There is no need to figure anything out if you want to make it for the holiday.
After grating the veggies, don't drain them. The extra liquid is used in the kugel.

# KISHUIM (ZUCCHINI) KUGEL

 10 minutes     60 minutes

## Ingredients:

- **kishuim or zucchini - 5**
- **onion - 2 large**
- **oil - 1/2 cup**
- **potato starch - 1 cup**
- **baking powder - 1 tablespoon**
- **parve chicken soup bouillon - 1 tablespoon**
- **salt - 1 teaspoon**

## Instructions:

1. **Grate onions and kishuim**
2. **Mix all ingredients together and pour into a baking pan**
3. **Bake at 375 degrees for 1 hour**

I like Israeli kishuim better than American zucchini. It has a much lighter flavor and I feel it works better in most recipes. Yes, it is one more reason to make Aliya (move to Israel). I have a kishuim kugel that I make during the year. This is very similar. I don't use water at all, and I use potato starch instead of flour. You can't really taste the difference between the two.

I have a separate food processor that I use for kugels. For me, it has totally been worth the investment.

# PEPPER SALAD

 10 minutes   50 minutes

## Ingredients:

- **bell peppers - 5 large, sliced in strips**
- **kosher salt - 1 teaspoon**
- **garlic - 3 cloves, chopped**
- **olive oil - 1 tablespoon**

## Instructions:

1. **Heat pot**
2. **Lower heat and add peppers and salt**
3. **Cook on low heat until the peppers release their juices, about 45 minutes**
4. **Add garlic and cook 5 more minutes**
5. **Remove from heat and add olive oil**
6. **Refrigerate and serve chilled**

This is a recipe that I got from my friend Ziza. She makes it practically every week. It's easy, low in fat, and everyone loves it. She says that it's important to use a good pot. Since you won't be cooking the peppers in oil, make sure to use a heavy, non-stick pot to get the job done right. It's helpful that the peppers release their own juices so that they don't stick to the pan.

Use lots of colors of peppers. It makes it beautifully colorful.

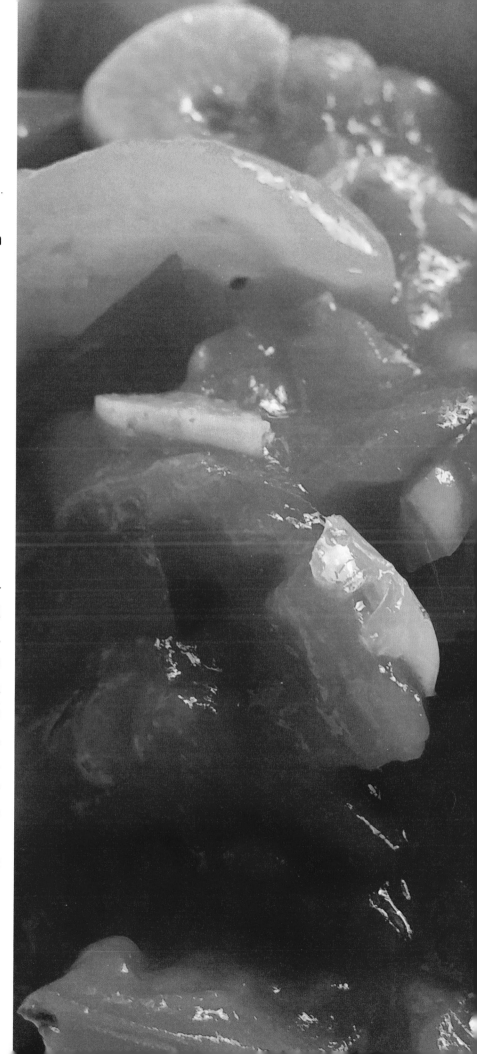

# SPINACH SALAD

 **5 minutes**

**Ingredients:**

- **spinach - 1 bag, fresh**
- **pecans - 1/2 cup, chopped**
- **raspberry preserves - 1/4 cup**
- **red wine vinegar - 1/4 cup**
- **craisins - 1/3 cup**

**Instructions:**

1. **Wash the leaves and dry them**
2. **Put preserves and vinegar in a salad dressing shaker and shake**
3. **Mix everything together**
4. **Serve immediately**

My husband doesn't usually touch anything made with the "S" word unless I sneak it in a way that he can't taste it or just doesn't notice that it's there. This salad he'll eat. I figure that if for no other reason, this makes this a worthy salad. This is an easy salad that everyone loves.

# POTATO SALAD

 15 minutes     30 minutes

## Ingredients:

- **potatoes - 5 large, cubed**
- **water - for boiling**
- **vegan mayonnaise - 1/2 cup**
- **pickles - 2, chopped**
- **onion - 1/4 cup, chopped**
- **carrot - 1, grated**
- **salt - to taste**

## Instructions:

1. **Boil potatoes in water until they are soft, but not mushy, about 10 minutes**
2. **Drain and let cool**
3. **Mix in a bowl with the rest of the ingredients**
4. **Serve warm or cold**

Now that I know how to make my own vegan mayonnaise, I'm having fun making food that I haven't eaten in a long time. Potato salad is one of those foods. It's funny what emotions come to play when you think about food. When I think about potato salad I think of picnics and pot luck meals with friends. Potato salad is just a happy food that brings people together.

If you don't have mayo, you can use oil (I like olive oil for this). It's pretty good, but it's not mayo.

# BAKED CARROTS

 **10 minutes**    **40 minutes**

**Ingredients:**

- **carrots - 8**
- **garlic - 3 cloves**
- **olive oil - 3 tablespoons**
- **kosher salt - 1 teaspoon**
- **thyme - 1/2 teaspoon**

**Instructions:**

1. **Preheat over to 400 degrees**
2. **Peel and slice carrots into sticks**
3. **Slice garlic**
4. **Mix all the ingredients together and place in a baking dish**
5. **Cover with tin foil and bake for 30 minutes**
6. **Uncover and cook for 10 more minutes**
7. **Serve warm**

I use a lot of carrots when I cook. I use them in kugels, kishke, soups and stews. I practically never just make carrots. I don't know why I don't. They are great by themselves. This dish is a savory side. I used to make candied carrots, but if I'm going to go sweet, I'll make tzimmes. This is a nice change.

One of the nice things about this dish is that you can serve it practically any time and to most people – it's vegan, and free of gluten, soy, sugar and nuts. I guess it's one of those foods that just brings people together.

# MATZO KUGEL

 30 minutes  30 minutes

## Ingredients:

- **matzo - 10 pieces**
- **water**
  *Savory version*
- **oil - 2 tablespoons**
- **mushrooms - 2 packages**
- **salt - 2 teaspoons**
  *Sweet version*
- **apples - 5, peeled and chopped**
- **raisins - 1/2 cup**
- **sugar - 1/2 cup**
- **cinnamon - 1 1/2 teaspoons**
- **vanilla - 1 teaspoon**

## Instructions:

1. **Break matzo into small pieces**
2. **Soak in water for 10-15 minutes and drain**
3. **For savory version: chop up mushrooms and onions and fry in oil until browned lightly**
4. **Mix together all the ingredients and place in oiled baking dish**
5. **Bake at 350 for 20-30 minutes until lightly browned on top**

My mom is the matzo kugel queen. She has been making matzo kugel every Passover for as long as I can remember. She makes two different types of kugel: a savory one with mushroom and a sweet one with apples and raisins. They are both amazing. I'm not sure which one I like more.

# RAW BEET SALAD

 **10 minutes**

**Ingredients:**

- beet - 1
- carrots - 2
- green apples - 2
- lemon juice - 1/2 lemon
- salt - to taste

**Instructions:**

1. Peel and grate beet, carrots and apple together
2. Add the rest of the ingredients
3. Mix well and serve

My friend Ziza, whom I like to think of as the salad queen, has come up with another one. This one is completely raw. There is no need to cook the beets.

I never thought of beets as a food to eat raw, but it really works here. Beets are just too hard to eat by themselves. Grating makes them manageable

Vegan Start

# SWEET POTATO AND PECAN CASSEROLE

 30 minutes　　 45 minutes

## Ingredients:

*Casserole*
- sweet potatoes - 4 medium
- brown sugar - 1/3 cup
- cinnamon - 1 teaspoon
- nutmeg - 1/2 teaspoon
- salt - 1/2 teaspoon

*Topping*
- pecans - 1/3 cup, chopped
- cinnamon - 1/2 teaspoon
- brown sugar - 1 tablespoon

## Instructions:

1. Peel, chop and boil sweet potatoes
2. Drain and mash the sweet potatoes when they are soft
3. Add the rest of the casserole ingredients
4. Pour into greased casserole dish
5. Mix topping ingredients together
6. Spread topping evenly over casserole
7. Bake at 350 degrees for 45 minutes
8. Serve warm

Every time that I make sweet potatoes I think that I should make them more often. Perhaps it's because they are so sweet I think of them more in the dessert category than something that I would eat during the main course. I find them very confusing that way.

This is really a Thanksgiving type of recipe. I've always thought of Passover as the Jewish Thanksgiving. Colonists came to America to escape European tyranny and Jews left Egypt to gain their freedom.

# MAINS

No one goes hungry in my house. The dishes in the next section are the main events.

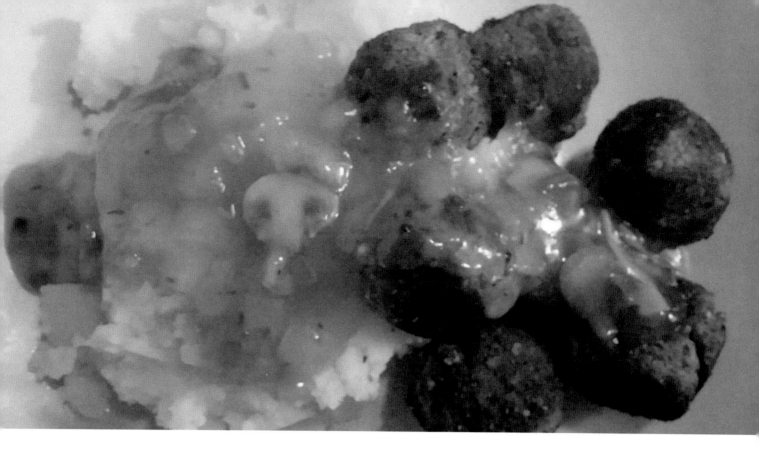

# "MEATBALLS"

 15 minutes     15 minutes

### Ingredients:

- walnuts - 2 cups
- shitake mushrooms - 2 cups
- garlic - 2 large cloves
- onion - 1/2 cup, chopped
- thyme - 1 teaspoon
- salt - 1/2 teaspoon
- matzo meal - 1/2 cup
- oil - for frying

### Instructions:

1. Process mushrooms, walnuts, garlic and onion in a blender
2. Add spices and matzo meal and mix thoroughly
3. Heat oil in a frying pan
4. Roll into small meatballs and fry in oil until all sides are browned
5. Serve warm

There has been some great progress in the world of vegan meat substitutions. Unfortunately, most of them are not Passover-friendly. I've made lots of different types of meatball recipes. Some use soy flakes. Others use gluten. I've even made them out of chickpeas. All of these are very problematic for Ashkenazi Jews during Passover. I had to come up with something different.

This is one of the many recipes that was inspired by raw cookbooks. This recipe is far from raw. I don't think that you could get less raw than frying something in olive oil. The inspiration is still there.

Walnuts and mushrooms are used to get that nice meaty taste. Try these with Passover spaghetti or eat with mashed potatoes and gravy.

# OVEN-FRIED MUSHROOMS

 10 minutes        30 minutes

## Ingredients:

- **mushrooms - 1 carton, sliced thinly**
- **potato starch - 1/2 cup**
- **olive oil - 1/4 cup**
- **water - 1/4 cup**
- **garlic - 1 tablespoon**
- **salt - 1 teaspoon**
- **matzo meal - 1 cup**

## Instructions:

1. **Pour potato starch in a Ziploc bag with mushrooms and shake them up so that all sides are coated**
2. **In a second Ziploc bag, add olive oil and water and shake coated mushrooms**
3. **In a separate bowl, add spices to matzo meal and make sure all sides of mushrooms are coated**
4. **Place mushrooms on a baking sheet and cook at 350 degrees for 20-30 minutes, until mushrooms are crisp**
5. **Serve warm with dipping sauce**

I was looking through my raw cookbook again and they had a recipe for mushroom calamari. Instead of cooking in the oven, they used a dehydrator to get the mushrooms nice and crisp. Because I wanted this recipe for Passover, I made a bunch of changes to it. They used flaxseeds as their coating, and I use matzo meal and potato starch – two very un-raw foods. No matter, it still comes out great and it takes a lot less time.

You can use any mushrooms you like for this. I used button white ones, but Portobello or shitake work well too.

# "SPAGHETTI" AND TOMATO SAUCE

 20 minutes     30 minutes

## Ingredients:

- **zucchini - 4 large, julienned**
- **olive oil - 2 tablespoons**
- **onion - 1 large, chopped**
- **mushrooms - 4 large, sliced thin**
- **garlic - 2 cloves, chopped**
- **oregano - 2 teaspoon**
- **salt - 1 teaspoon**
- **tomato paste - 2 containers**
- **water - 2 cups**

## Instructions:

1. **Heat oil in a large frying pan**
2. **Add onions, mushrooms and garlic, and fry on medium heat until onions are translucent**
3. **Add spices, tomato paste and water, and mix well**
4. **Cook on a medium heat for 15 more minutes**
5. **Blanch the zucchini**
6. **Serve like regular pasta**

I don't eat raw food on a regular basis. I do have a couple of raw recipe books that inspire me. They are particularly useful when it comes to Pesach time. That's the first time that I saw kishuim (zucchini) being used in place of wheat spaghetti. And so, my Pesach spaghetti was born.

I make this tomato sauce throughout the year. You can keep the zucchini raw if you like. I blanch it for a minute or two.

# RATATOUILLE

 20 minutes         30 minutes

## Ingredients:

- olive oil - 2 tablespoons
- onion - 1 large, chopped
- mushrooms - 4, sliced
- garlic - 2 tablespoons, chopped
- carrots - 2 large, chopped
- bell pepper - 1 large, chopped
- zucchini - 2 large, chopped
- eggplant - 1 medium, chopped
- tomato paste - 1 container
- water - 1/2 cup
- oregano - 1 teaspoon
- basil - 1/2 teaspoon
- bay leaves - 2
- salt - 1 teaspoon

## Instructions:

1. Heat oil in a large frying pan
2. Add vegetables, one at a time, cooking each of them down before adding the next
3. Add spices, tomato paste and water and simmer for 15 minutes
4. Serve with mashed potatoes

Ratatouille is another recipe that I've been making forever, even before the movie came out. Even though ratatouille has French origins, I think my version is more like its Italian cousin. I use oregano, basil and tomato paste.

I got this recipe from my mother years ago. For me, this is really comfort food. We used to eat it as a side dish, but there really is no reason that it can't be a main dish all on its own.

I put each of the vegetables in one at a time. While the first goes in, I prepare the next. There's no waiting time.

# TZIMMES

 20 minutes          30 minutes

## Ingredients:

- olive oil - 2 tablespoons
- onion - 1 large, chopped
- carrots - 5-6, sliced
- sweet potatoes - 2, cubed
- prunes - 1 cup
- date honey - 1/3 cup
- water - 1/3 cup
- cinnamon - 1 teaspoon
- salt - 1/2 teaspoon

## Instructions:

1. Heat oil in a pot
2. Add onions and cook until translucent
3. Add carrots and cook for 5 minutes
4. Add sweet potatoes and cook for another 2 minutes
5. Add the rest of the ingredients and stir until veggies are covered with honey
6. Let stew on a low flame until sweet potatoes are cooked through and prunes are soft
7. Serve warm

One of my no-brainer things to make on Passover is Tzimmes. If you don't know what Tzimmes is, it's basically a sweet stew. I make this twice a year – on Rosh Hashana and Passover. This is a holiday staple in our house.

# MUSHROOM BURGERS

 15 minutes      10 minutes

## Ingredients:

- olive oil - 2 tablespoons
- onion - 1 large, chopped
- mushrooms - 1 1/2 containers
- cashews - 1 cup
- ketchup - 1/2 cup
- matzo meal - 1/2 cup
- salt - 1/2 teaspoon

## Instructions:

1. Heat oil in a frying pan to medium heat
2. Add onions and mushrooms and cook until onions translucent and caramelized. If the pan starts to dry out, you can add water
3. Remove from heat and let cool.
4. Place cashews in a food processor and process until coarsely ground
5. Add the rest of the ingredients to the food processor and process until blended
6. Shape mixture into patties and grill on each side for about 10 minutes
7. Serve

I always have fun making things with mushrooms. They have a really neat texture and they taste really good. They also make a wonderful meat substitute. I use them for my chopped liver recipe, and now I'm using them for burgers. Burgers are just one of those foods that it's really hard to live without. The truth of the matter is that once you have the main ingredients down, you can season it however you like. In Israel, I've seen a lot of restaurants put parsley in their burgers. I'm not that into that, but if that's what floats your boat, go for it.

A nice thing about making burgers like this is that you don't have to worry about undercooking them. None of the ingredients actually need to be cooked to be consumed so there is totally no worry of salmonella. Back in the day, that's something that I always worried about when going to some of those fast food burger places. Hamburgers are among those foods that often bring us happy memories of childhood. These burgers provide those memories without the ham … uh, beef.

# MUSHROOM STEAKS

 2 hours          25 minutes

## Ingredients:

- portobello mushrooms - 1 package
- garlic - 2 cloves, chopped
- olive oil - 1/4 cup
- water - 1/4 cup
- thyme - 1 teaspoon

## Instructions:

1. Gently remove stems from mushrooms
2. In a Ziploc bag, add all the ingredients
3. Let mushrooms marinate for a couple of hours
4. Heat oven to 350 degrees
5. Remove mushrooms from marinade and roast on a cookie sheet for 20 minutes
6. Flip mushrooms & cook for 5 more minutes
7. Serve warm

I use mushrooms in so many dishes, that I think I may one day turn into a mushroom. Different mushrooms have different flavors. Portobello mushrooms have a wonderful meaty flavor and are nice and big, so you feel like you are having a juicy piece of meat. (Well maybe not exactly, but it is pretty close).

You only use the caps for this recipe. I save the stems and use them in other dishes. Waste not, want not.

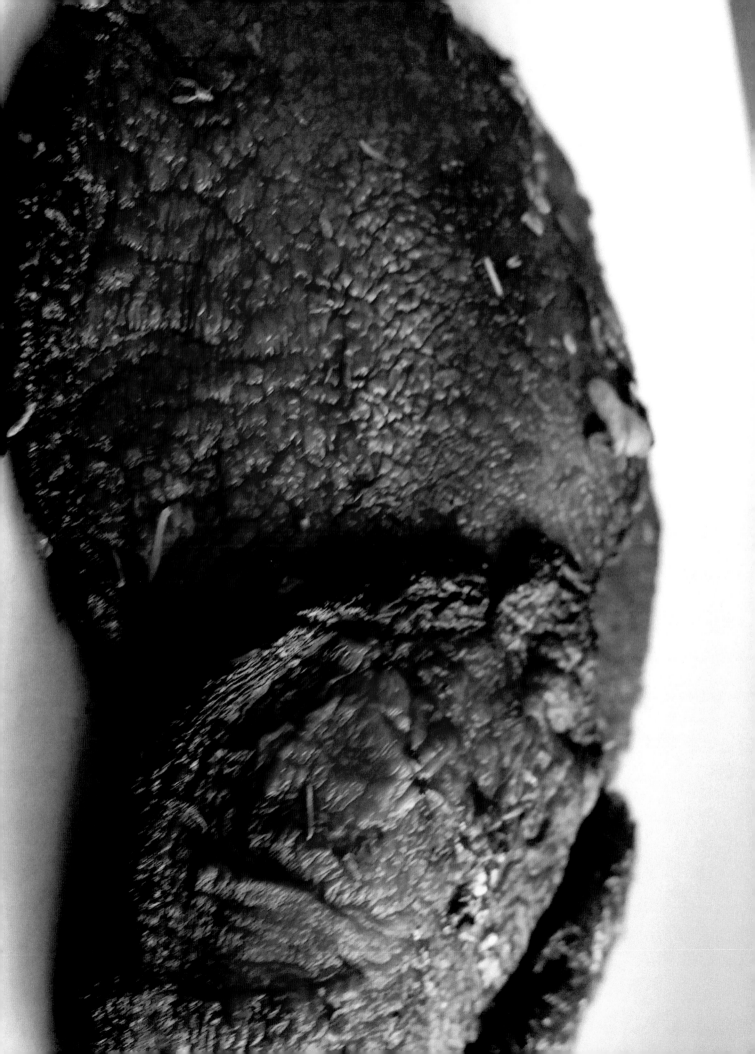

# GNOCCHI

 40 minutes     60 minutes

## Ingredients:

- potatoes - 5 large
- matzo meal - 2 cups, finely ground
- salt - 1 teaspoon
- water for boiling

## Instructions:

1. Boil potatoes in their skins for 40-50 minutes, check with a toothpick to see if their soft enough
2. Let potatoes cool a bit (should still be warm) and peel off skins
3. Put potatoes through a potato ricer (if you have one) or mash
4. Mix thoroughly with matzo meal and salt until you have a dough. Depending on the size of your potatoes, you may need more or less matzo meal
5. Let sit for 10 minutes
6. Roll dough in batches so that they are in long strings, about 1/2 inch in diameter
7. Cut strand into 3/4 inch segments
8. Roll each segment on a fork, pressing into the fork with your thumb and rolling them down
9. Boil water
10. Add gnocchi to it and boil until the gnocchi rises
11. Remove from water with slotted spoon
12. Serve with tomato or pesto sauce

Gnocchi is one of those foods that I enjoy making. I can't lie – it's a lot of work. There are a lot of steps that take time. When I first started rolling the gnocchi, I thought it was going to take forever. The first few take a bit of time, but once you get your groove, it all goes much faster.

We eat a ton of potatoes on Pesach, but I think this recipe is a nice change from the norm. I made it using matzo meal that I put in my blender to make it extra fine, but I'm sure that potato starch would work too.

Some people boil the potatoes, others bake them. If you boil them (like I do) make sure that you boil them in their skins and only remove the skins after. If you don't, the potatoes get too watery and you'll have mush.

# QUINOA MUSHROOM PILAF

 10 minutes  30 minutes

## Ingredients:

- olive oil - 2 tablespoons
- onions - 1 large, chopped
- mushrooms - 1 package, chopped
- garlic - 2 cloves, chopped
- quinoa- 1 1/2 cups
- water - 3 cups
- thyme - 1 teaspoon
- salt 1 teaspoon

## Instructions:

1. Heat oil and add chopped vegetables
2. Cook until onions are translucent
3. Rinse quinoa well
4. Add quinoa and cook until lightly browned
5. Add spices and liquid and bring to boil
6. Lower heat and let simmer for about 15 minutes, until all the liquid is absorbed
7. Serve warm

I used to shy away from making quinoa. When I first tried it out it came out bitter. I learned later that it is important to rinse the quinoa well before you use it. It might be overkill, but just to make sure, I rinse my quinoa three times.

Quinoa is actually a very healthy food. It's full of protein, even though it acts like a carbohydrate.

You can use it practically everywhere you use rice.

Luckily, this food was found in South America. If it were found in Europe, the rabbis might have put it in the category of kitnyot, making it not allowed for Ashkenazim on Passover.

# SOUTHERN FRIED OKRA

 20 minutes    20 minutes

## Ingredients:

- okra - 1 package (400 grams)
- almond milk - 1/2 cup
- vinegar - 1 teaspoon
- matzo meal - 3/4 cup
- almond meal - 1/2 cup
- hot paprika - 1 teaspoon
- salt - 1 teaspoon
- oil - for frying

## Instructions:

1. Defrost and dry okra well
2. Mix milk with vinegar
3. Mix dry ingredients
4. Dunk okra into milk
5. Coat well with dry mixture
6. Deep fry until golden brown

I like to look for different flavors to make Passover a bit more exciting. I have always found okra to be one of the more interesting tastes. It has a bit of a sweet flavor.

My Iraqi grandmother used to make okra all the time. She made it in a tomato sauce, which we all loved. My brother still goes on about how my

Savta Flora z"l was the best cook ever.

I thought that I would go in a different direction. Instead of going the sweet direction, I thought I'd do sweet and salty. I am from the south, after all. I lived in both Memphis

and Dallas, so I need to connect to those roots too. This is my way of remembering my Savta Flora.

# DESSERTS

I have to admit that this was the most fun part of the book for me. For my family too. I have a horrible sweet tooth. And I love chocolate. Both of these are taken care of in the recipes in this section. I hope that you enjoy eating them as much as I enjoyed making them!

# PASSOVER TURTLE BARS

 10 minutes   12 minutes

## Ingredients:

- matzo - 1 piece
- margarine - 150 grams
- brown sugar - 3/4 cup
- pecans - 1 1/2 cups, chopped
- salt - pinch
- chocolate chips - 1 cup
- slivered almonds - 3 tablespoons

## Instructions:

1. Line a pan with baking paper
2. Place matzo in the pan
3. Melt the margarine, brown sugar, pecans and salt in a sauce pan.
4. Bring to a boil, lower heat and let cook 2 minutes
5. Pour mixture on the piece of matzo and bake at 350 degrees for 1 minute
6. Take out of oven and sprinkle with chocolate chips
7. Return to oven for 2 more minutes
8. Remove from oven and spread chocolate on the pecan mixture
9. Sprinkle with almonds
10. Cut while hot
11. Let cool and serve

I make a lot of different types of desserts for Passover. Two of them are particularly decadent. This one and a chocolate torte that I make every year. This is by far the easier of the two. You use a piece of matzoh to hold it all together. The truth is it really is a pity to only eat them one week a year.

I don't even bother with a bowl to mix these up. Everything can be mixed in a sauce pan.

# CHOCOLATE TRUFFLES

 **15 minutes**

## Ingredients:

- **dates - 1/2 cup**
- **almonds - 1 cup**
- **vanilla - 1 teaspoon**
- **agave syrup - 1 teaspoon**
- **water - 3 tablespoons**
- **cocoa powder - 2 tablespoons**
- **salt - pinch**
- **coconut flakes - about 1/3 cup - to roll the balls in**

## Instructions:

1. **Grind almonds in a food processor until well ground**
2. **Add dates and grind some more**
3. **Add the rest of the ingredients and process until you have a thick paste**
4. **Roll into balls about 1 1/2 centimeters in diameter**
5. **Roll in coconut flakes**

My cousin Toby and her husband have stopped eating sugar (some people have the craziest diet restrictions :-)). When I say stopped I mean they have no sugar at all. They check the labels of the food that they bring into the house. Everything they cook and bake is without any refined sugar. That said – they don't go completely sweet free. They sometimes eat foods made with other sweeteners. Besides agave, stevia, date honey and maple syrup, dates by themselves work wonderfully in recipes. I've used them for raw pie bottoms, and when I make almond milk, they gave a nice sweetness and thickness to the milk. The juicier dates are the Medjool dates. They're the ones to use.

When Toby and her family came to us for Passover, she made chocolate truffles out of dates. That's what inspired this recipe.

These don't have a heavy date taste. The dates are there to give texture and sweetness.

I've seen a lot of recipes that use walnuts. For me, walnuts are a very heavy nut and sometimes have a bit of a bitter taste to them. I like using walnuts with mushrooms as a meat substitute, but in this recipe I prefer to use almonds.

Warning: Your hands will be very sticky while your roll the truffles. I thought about putting on rubber gloves before I started, but I don't think that would have helped much. You can try wetting your hands a bit between truffles, but don't use too much water or the truffles will get mushy and it will be harder to roll them in the coconut flakes.

These guys are fun to make. I hope you enjoy them!

# RAW CHOCOLATE MOUSSE

 **14 minutes**

**Ingredients:**

- **avocados - 2 large**
- **almond milk - 2 tablespoons**
- **cocoa powder - 1/4 cup**
- **maple syrup - 1/2 cup**
- **vanilla - 1 teaspoon**

**Instructions:**

1. **Remove peel and pit from avocados**
2. **Put everything in a blender**
3. **Process until smooth**
4. **Serve chilled**

This is another one of my raw-friendly recipes. I like to find new recipes that are sugar-free for when my cousins come. This is one of the stranger ones. To get the creaminess of the mousse, you use a very unlikely ingredient: avocado. The first time I saw this recipe, I thought, what are these people trying to prove? I was intrigued and had to try it. It was surprisingly good.

Don't be afraid of the avocados. Just make sure that they are super ripe before you start. If not, they won't blend well and you'll be left with a super mess.

# MACADAMIA NUT BANANA CREAM

 **10 minutes**

## Ingredients:

- **macadamia nuts - 3 cups**
- **coconut oil - 3 tablespoons**
- **bananas - 3 large**
- **vanilla - 1 teaspoon**
- **maple syrup - 1/4 cup**

## Instructions:

1. **Place ingredients in a strong food processor**
2. **Process until smooth**
3. **Serve chilled**

I love making nut creams. I find it really cool that you can take something hard, like a nut, and turn it into something completely different. This is a raw recipe, meaning that nothing here is cooked. I think that makes it even cooler.

This recipe calls for coconut oil. You can pick it up in any health food store in Israel. In Israel, you may need to buy the coconut oil before Passover. because a lot of health food stores close during the week of Chol Hamoed.

Coconut oil is solid when cool. If heated, it melts like butter. Cool it again and it turns back into a solid.

# ALMOND CHOCOLATE MOUSSE

 **20 minutes**

## Ingredients:

- **almonds - 1 cup**
- **agave syrup - 1/4 cup**
- **chocolate chips - 1/2 cup**
- **almond milk - 1 cup**
- **salt - pinch**
- **vanilla - 1 teaspoon**

## Instructions:

1. **Soak almonds in boiling water for at least 2 hours**
2. **Peel almonds and soak overnight**
3. **Process almonds and agave syrup in food processor or blender**
4. **Bring milk to boil**
5. **Lower heat and add chocolate, stirring until all the chocolate is melted**
6. **Add milk mixture to the food processor and blend until smooth**
7. **Pour into cups and refrigerate until mousse sets**
8. **Eat**

A lot of people ask me "don't I miss [fill in the blank with non-vegan food]?" There's very little out there for which I haven't found substitutes. I mean, I've made everything from ribs to cheese cake, and all have been vegan. It's true, that some of these mock foods are more successful than others, but I really can't say that I miss anything. It could be that I'm lucky that I would never eat milk chocolate when dark chocolate was around. And I've always been a fan of the lighter fare over meat dishes. In the past, when I would make cholent with meat, I'd only eat the beans and veggies and leave over the rest for everyone else. For me, the hardest thing about being vegan is the lack of convenience food.

My recipe for mousse is not something that you can do at a moment's notice. It needs planning and preparing before you're able to enjoy the finished product. Although it takes time it is not difficult to make. You know how they say "good things come to those who wait?" Well in this case, it's totally true.

You can use already blanched almonds to save some time.

The main reason the almonds need to soak for so long is that they need to get nice and soft so they turn to mush when you process them. If you do it too soon they can make the mousse gritty-feeling – not the nice smooth sensation that you're going for when you think of mousse.

If you're having guests and want to impress them, this is the right way to go. You can even throw in a splash of rum to make it more fun if you're going for really fancy. It's really superb.

# CHOCOLATE CHIP COOKIES

 **10 minutes**   🕐 **15 minutes**

## Ingredients:

- **matzo meal - 1 cup**
- **sugar - 1/2 cup**
- **potato starch - 1/4 cup**
- **baking soda - 1 teaspoon**
- **salt - 1 teaspoon**
- **cinnamon - 1 teaspoon**
- **oil - 1/2 cup**
- **almond milk - 2/3 cup**
- **vanilla - 2 teaspoons**
- **chocolate chips - 3/4 cup**

## Instructions:

1. **Add all ingredients to a bowl except the chocolate chips and mix well**
2. **Add chocolate chips and mix**
3. **Place heaping teaspoons of batter on a cookie sheet and flatten with your palm**
4. **Bake at 350 degrees for 10-15 minutes**
5. **Cool on rack and eat**

The first vegan recipe that I ever posted on my blog was for chocolate chip cookies. You can probably guess that they are very dear to my heart. We never used the cookie dough in the fridge section growing up.

The kids love these cookies. I've made them during the year and they always all get gobbled up. If you can get your kids to happily eat Passover cookies during the year, you know you got a good thing going.

# ALMOND COOKIES

 10 minutes       20 minutes

## Ingredients:

- margarine - 1 1/2 cups
- powdered sugar - 1 1/3 cups
- vanilla - 6 teaspoons
- almond extract - 3 teaspoons
- cinnamon - 2 teaspoons
- salt - 1/2 teaspoon
- matzo meal - 3 cups
- almonds - 1 cup, ground
- powdered sugar - for dusting

## Instructions:

1. Combine margarine, sugar, vanilla, almond extract, cinnamon, and salt
2. Add matzo meal and mixed well
3. Stir in ground almonds
4. Shape into teaspoon size balls of dough
5. Roll into powdered sugar and place on greased baking sheet
6. Bake at 350 degrees for 20 minutes

When I made these cookies I thought they were really good. What really surprised me was when my non-vegan friend had one and said that they don't taste like Passover cookies. I think that is the biggest compliment that any Passover food could get. The fact that it's vegan just puts it over the top.

These cookies use a lot of margarine. In general I try to avoid making margarine-based foods. Since Passover is only one week a year, I figure how much damage could it do?

# APPLE CAKE

 20 minutes     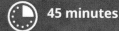 45 minutes

## Ingredients:

*Batter*
- apple sauce - 1 cup
- oil - 1/2 cup
- sugar - 1/2 cup
- matzo meal - 1 1/2 cups
- potato starch - 1/2 cup
- baking powder - 1 teaspoon
- vanilla - 1 teaspoon
- salt - 1/2 teaspoon
- water - 2/3 cup

*Filling*
- apples - 4 large, peeled and thinly sliced
- brown sugar - 1/2 cup
- cinnamon - 2 teaspoons

*Topping*
- nuts - 1/4 cup, ground
- brown sugar - 1/4 cup

## Instructions:

1. Beat together apple sauce, oil, sugar, matzo meal, potato starch, baking powder, vanilla, salt and water together in a bowl
2. Line the bottom of a greased pan with half of the mixture
3. Toss together apples, cinnamon and 1/2 cup brown sugar
4. Layer apple mixture in pan
5. Cover with remaining batter
6. Mix together 1/4 c. brown sugar and ground nuts and sprinkle on top of batter
7. Bake for 45 minutes at 350 degrees

During the year, it's hard to find baked goods in your local grocery store that are vegan. On Passover, it's impossible. Everything, and I mean everything, is made with eggs. It's crazy. I have one old recipe book where each cake requires at least 7 eggs, and sometimes as many as 12. Instead of eggs, I added extra apple sauce to keep it all together.

This is the Passover version of apple crumble.

It's more like bars than actual cake. I mean, how wrong can you go with apples, sugar and cinnamon?

just one piece of cake...

# CHOCOLATE TORTE

 10 minutes       20 minutes

## Ingredients:

*Crust*
- **pecans - 1 cup**
- **walnuts - 1 cup**
- **brown sugar - 1/2 cup**
- **margarine - 3 tablespoons**

*Torte*
- **almond milk - 2 cups**
- **chocolate chips - 2 1/2 cups**
- **vanilla - 1 teaspoon**
- **potato starch - 3 tablespoons**

## Instructions:

1. **Put nuts, sugar and margarine in blender**
2. **Place in bottom of a tart pan, spread out and mash down**
3. **Bake at 350 degrees for 10 minutes**
4. **Melt milk, chocolate chips and vanilla in a pot**
5. **Slowly put in potato starch and bring to boil**
6. **Pour into tart pan and cool in fridge until it hardens**

This is a recipe that I make once a year. There's no real reason not to make it more often, I just like it to be special for Pesach. I started making it years ago, when I started making my own almond milk. It's probably good that I only make this once a year – it is so crazy decadent that it takes a whole year to atone for eating it.

This was one of my first attempts at making a Passover dessert recipe after I became vegan. I'm really happy with the results.

# COCONUT MACAROONS

 5 minutes        15 minutes

## Ingredients:

- shredded coconut - 1 cup
- almond flour - 1/3 cup
- maple syrup - 2 tablespoons
- vanilla - 1 teaspoon
- almond milk - 5 tablespoons
- salt - pinch

## Instructions:

1. Heat oven to 350 degrees.
2. Combine all ingredients in a food processor, except the coconut and process until fine.
3. Add the coconut and process until mixed in.
4. Roll batter into 3/4 inch balls and place them on a cookie sheet.
5. Bake for 15 minutes or until golden brown

Most Israelis don't know what the Passover macaroons that we used to get in the Streit's cylindrical container are. When you say macaroon in Israel, it means these pretty little sandwich cookies, not the Passover fare. I don't know about now, but at least when I was a kid, the American version of these only came out around Passover time. They were such a symbol of Passover in our house!

I think now you can now get macaroons here in some of the more American supermarkets. That's not really particularly helpful to me because they are full of eggs. Aquafava has been all the rage this year, and a lot of people are using it to make their egg white replacements. I've seen it being used in mayonnaise and meringues. Aquafava would be a perfect substitute if I were not Ashekenazi. (It's the liquid from cans of beans, like chickpeas).

I make almond milk every year for Passover. After I dry out the processed almonds from the milk in the oven, I grind them up and use them for almond flour. That flour is perfect to use for this recipe. It's good that we go through a lot of almond milk!

Small plate for tastey dessert

# POACHED PEARS

 10 minutes    40 minutes

### Ingredients:

- **pears - 4**
- **water - 4 cups**
- **silan - 1/3 cup**
- **sugar - 1/4 cup**
- **ground ginger - 1 teaspoon**
- **cinnamon - 1 stick**
- **vanilla - 1/2 teaspoon**
- **salt - 1 pinch**

### Instructions:

1. **Peel and core pears**
2. **Bring water, silan, sugar, ginger, cinnamon, vanilla and salt to a boil**
3. **Add pears and simmer for 20-30 minutes, until pears are tender**
4. **Serve warm**

I have a pear tree that I see outside my dining room table. I love looking at it all year long. It starts blooming after Tu B'shvat and the pears become ripe around Passover. Pretty convenient if you want to make poached pears.

Pears by themself are good, but when you poach them they become even better. One thing that I really like about this dessert is how pretty it looks.

# THANK YOU

*I want to thank everyone that has given me support and allowed me to create this cookbook. It all started with a blog a few years ago. The encouragement that I got from my family and friends to share my recipes with the world put me down this road.*

*Food is something to be shared with people you love. I am very lucky to have a wonderful family that has shared in making and eating the food.*

*This is a Passover Cookbook. That means that I have been cooking Passover food for months before Passover. My family members have been my taste testers. For others, Passover is just one week a year. In our house that just hasn't been the case. Thank you family for suffering through all of my trials and errors. Lucky for them there were more successes than failures. They have been the best guinea pigs anyone could hope for. Their honest critique has helped me become a better cook.*

*I need to thank my mom. I learned most of what I know about cooking from her. Perhaps most importantly, to love the process, not be afraid to take chances and share your successes.*

*I'd like to thank my husband for editing every recipe in this book and on my blog. Putting it all together, especially the second edition, was a lot more work than I expected. Without his support and love, I don't know if this edition would have seen the light of day.*

# ABOUT ME

Hi, I'm Rena. Ever since I became a vegan, close to 6 years ago, I've wanted to write a cookbook to help other vegans not fear Passover. I was freaking out before my first vegan Passover. That was before Ashkenazim could eat quinoa, but even so, my first vegan Passover went off mostly without any hitches. I did eat more Matzo than I usually do, but otherwise, everything was cool. I did not go hungry.

Every year I expand my recipe list. I've had a lot of fun experimenting. Most of the time I've been pretty successful. There are the occasional flops. It took me forever to come up with a good crepe recipe.

All the recipes in this cookbook can be eaten by Ashkenazim and Sephardim alike. I know that I could probably get a heter for eating kitniyot (legumes, like beans and rice), but I've never tried.  Most of my kids are vegetarian and my husband is an omnivore, and I'm not going to spend a lot of time just cooking for myself.

I started writing for Vegan Start (http://veganstart.com) in 2010, shortly after I became vegan. I like to joke that becoming vegan is all my daughter's fault. She was reading the book Eating Animals by Jonathan Safran Foer. She told me what was going on in the factory farming industry, so I read the book for myself. It was a complete eye opener. I didn't just take the book's word, I did some research myself.

I've been a huge animal lover all my life. I get that from my mother's side. My mom (who is also vegan) and I have created a website to share information about pets. It's called The Pet Wiki (http://thepetwiki.com/). I (with help from Eliora, a wonderful programmer) do the technical stuff on the site and she takes care of most of the content. It's a wiki site, so people can add and edit content. We also have a great Q and A section where people can ask and get answers to their pet-related questions.

I live in Eli, a town north of Jerusalem. I share my home with my husband, my children, one dog, three cats and a sun conure. It can be a pretty noisy place sometimes. Two of the cats and the dog were adopted from the JSPCA. I've had the pleasure of working with the JSPCA, trying to help them get animals adopted. Eliora and I (mostly Eliora) built their website (that's what we do). You can see it at http://jspca.org.il/.

Made in the USA
Las Vegas, NV
24 February 2022

44485458R00057